AFTERTHOUGHT
A Collection of Poetry

LINDA ST. JOHN

Copyright © 2011 by Linda St. John Los Angeles, California
All Rights Reserved
Printed and Bound in the United States of America

Published and Distributed by:
Professional Publishing House
1424 W. Manchester Ave., Suite B
Los Angeles, CA 90047
www.professionalpublishinghouse.com
Drrosie@Drrosie.com
323-750-3592

Jacket photograph by Diamond Dust Photography
Cover Design: Cynthia Bluford
Interior Design: Caldonia Joyce
                Visual Bridge Designs

First Printing, April 2011
10 9 8 7 6 5 4 3 2 1
ISBN 978-0-9834444-0-4

Publisher's Note
All rights reserved. No part of this book may be reproduced in whole or in part, in any form or by any means, electronic or mechanical, including photocopying, recording or by any information storage and retrieval system, without permission in writing from the author. Address inquiries to: lindastjohn1000@gmail.com

ACKNOWLEDGEMENTS

Thank you Lord for the gift!

Thanks for loving me past my flaws
Mayeer, Mone-yaa, Gabrielle and Cherish Halliburton,
Mother, Ike, Michael and Lawrence

Thank you my unsung heroes
Debra K. Alfred, Paris Clutchette-Martin, Doris Brown,
Beverly McBee, Heavenor Hemmans and Dr. Rosie Milligan

My heroes
President Barack Obama, Michael Eric Dyson, Cornel West,
Tavis Smiley, Tyler Perry, Steve Harvey and Michael Baisden

My she-roes
First Lady Michelle Obama, Dr. Maya Angelou,
Oprah Winfrey, Cathy Hughes, Terry McMillan,
and Toni Morrison

What an honor to sit among these beautiful Queens
Cynthia Bluford, Charlene Bholanath, Desiree Zimmerman,
Mary Shelley, Teretha Bankhead, Renee McMullen, Patty McNeely
and Denise Estelle

I'm so grateful to
Antoine Lee
for his editing skills, a million thanks!

Love you JP,
thanks for your support

Thanks for the positive energy and encouragement
Kevin Jackson and Andre Maddux

I'm so proud of my play "brother" and gifted musician
Phil Mosley

*I'm grateful to have worked with some of the most
beautiful and brilliant people*
Carol Rose Schwartz, Ronald Mayhew, Howard Katz,
Jennifer Anderson, Darren Embry, Ismail Malam, Tyrone Jones,
Kay Swikart, Theresa Borel, Michelle Blackwell, Gio Baumann,
Parissa Saed, Seymour Litwin, Justine Sliwka, Amir Eshkol,
Jake Helgren, Cathy Kyriakou, Shanon Fraser, Wendy Gantt,
Virginia Tomogin, Pauline Gates, Rodger Watkins,
Richard Quinones, Cani Gonzalez, Tonita Hardy, and Ralph Garcia

Finally, a heartfelt thanks to all those whom I may have forgotten

ABOUT THE AUTHOR

Linda St. John was born in Columbia, Missouri. She spent hours fueling her imagination by getting lost in reading. However, it was her Mother's love of soap opera's that birthed the seed for storytelling. Linda was instructed to watch and relay what had transpired between the colorful characters; it was later that she realized this helped shape her gift.

Shortly thereafter, the family relocated to Los Angeles, California. It was during her early adolescent years that she discovered Dr. Maya Angelou's writings which made a huge impression. But it was in high school that a creative writing paper captured the attention of her English teacher who suggested she become a writer. Although the seed was planted, she lacked focus and direction. Soon afterward Linda became pregnant, pushed her dreams aside and sought to make a living as a single parent. In order to deal with the demands of life, she began to reflect by journaling.

As time passed she explored writing lyrics and then poetry; one of which was published. In the meantime she met and developed friendships with other writers which sharpened her writing skills. Linda has written short stories, screenplays and two novels, which will be published this year along with the collection of poetry, "Afterthought."

FOREWORD

When Linda St. John asked me to write the foreword, I was honored and excited. In the twenty years of knowing Linda, I've had the pleasure to read not only her present writings but also her earlier work. She is socially conscious, intelligent, beautiful, insightful and filled with ideas and thoughts about life and relationships. From the very first time she shared her writings, there was no doubt she would one day become a published writer. Linda is talented, gifted, honest and has a voice the world needs to hear. Her writings are reflections of truth, passion, beauty, inspiration, love, unselfishness and she has an uncanny way of baring her soul.

Afterthought provides the reader with a clear indication that Ms. St. John possesses the ability to pull you into her world by shaking you to the core. Afterthought touches your heart and soul. From the first poem "Every Now and Then" – which made me reflect upon love, past mistakes or about getting it right – it offsets an array of emotions. I have often been told great writing makes you sit up and take notice while looking within — in to the why's, how's and what if's.

"I Shall Be" – transports you to a place and time inspiring you to try something different and be all that you can.... I found myself getting lost and swept away within the poems – going in and out of time – my life, remembering special moments, past loves, or just getting lost in nostalgia. I was mesmerized by the words that grabbed a hold of my conscious and heart, making me feel as if I was sixteen years old again.

"In Love's Moment" – was short, sweet and straight to the point; prompting me to want to know who is that man and is there one for me? I felt as if I was experiencing all of these amazing sensations.

FOREWORD

Afterthought is smooth, modern, old fashioned, provocative, bold, spiritual and downright brilliant. Ms. St. John has a style of writing where the words seem to dance across the pages, embracing and pulling you in. The manner in which Linda tells each story evokes thoughts, sorrow, love, disappointment, joy or pain – makes you want to cheer; stand up for the hero or heroine.

Ms. St. John's net is laid out. As you read these little masterpieces – enjoy getting lost in each poem, grab a hold of love, power, adventure, or pursue happiness.

Afterthought left me in awe of someone I have known for many years. I'm proud to have this up and coming writer as a dear, personal friend. From start to finish Afterthought will pull you into different worlds until you have read the last word. When I read the last poem, I begged for more.

Afterthought will capture your mind, heart and spirit. It will bring tears, laughter and you'll fall in love over and over again. At times, I thought about the social directives, wondering what can I do – and when will I begin?

Or, I just want to do nothing but live and love. I laughed at the gestures and innuendos, got misty eyed at the notion of failed love and found courage in new love. I hung in there and took the journey through Linda's imagination. Afterthought will be remembered long after the book is placed on the coffee table or on your book shelf. Long after you have sat around with a glass of red wine and discussed Afterthought with your friends and colleagues.

— Debra K. Alfred

PREFACE

Many years ago I started writing poetry as a way to process my feelings. It was very therapeutic; I enjoyed expressing myself in a positive format. I tapped into my life well; was amazed at the internal issues buried deep within my soul. I cannot explain what is released during the writing process, but it is very liberating. You feel as if you've touched on something very special and spiritual. I am humbled and honored that God is so gracious in bestowing such a beautiful gift. It is my desire that you can feel what I'm trying to convey; as these poems are deeply personal.

CONTENTS

Now and Then   15

Silence of Passion   17

Chocolate Lover   18

Imagination   19

Thunder in My Bones   20

Journey   21

Menfolks   23

Dusk   24

African Violet   25

Rhythm of a Drag   26

In Love's Moment   27

More than Friends, Less than Lovers   28

Sista Maya   30

Afterthought   31

Kissing my Soul   33

Sweet Tears in Bitter Coffee   35

Mama's Eyes   37

I Remember Love   39

CONTENTS

I Shall Be….. 40

Lover's Point 42

October 43

Lost in You 44

Essence 45

Now and Then

At times a man doesn't know when to hold you
   you know...
   every now and then
   when he scolds you for not being on top of the game
   of loving him
Sometimes a man doesn't know when to say I love you
   you know..
   when you really need to hear it
   to arrest doubts of insecurity
once in awhile a man wants to be one just for fun
   you know...
   every now and then
   when you need to feel his passion
   but instead stroke his ego
Occasionally a man just does'nt have a clue
   of what it takes to glue
   your heart back together again
   after a bad relationship
   you know...
   every now and then
   when you need a shoulder to cry upon
   but he's out with his boys
From time to time a man doesn't know how to be a friend
   when
   you'd rather chat or cuddle
   but he's into the football huddle
   you know...
   every now and then....

Seasons

Lust lurked in the shadows
as we stole kisses in secret
a summer passion parade
was over before it started....
along comes troublesome fall, dreary and gray
rain masquerades as tears
lost my summer love, now
I
stand
alone
wrapped in a blanket of emptiness
Winter around the corner
colder
lines on my face
older
the winds of change blew us
away
however, I'm stronger now
as Spring steps in, pretty, crisp
my hopeful heart
anticipates
love ...again..
in this season

Silence of Passion

I strutted up the driveway
noticed him awaiting my arrival
arm propped up in the doorway
cigarette dangling from chocolate thin lips
ashes about to fall
like I fell for him
I stepped to him, removed the cancer stick
substituted it with a sugar-drenched kiss
however,
his lips were dry not ready for mine
disappointed I smashed it with my black sexy pumps
silently wishing it was his heart
gazing into his big, brown eyes
searching for answers in our love dance
Is it over?
I scanned his tattooed body, realizing the pain he endured
did he recognize our drama?
Could he understand? Or was he as cold as the night air?
he showered me with love, now
all I have is dryness in the desert
tumbleweeds blew our dreams away
he grabbed me, held me tight
my body froze with fear
I was delighted in the
silence of his passion

Chocolate Lover

I like mine with a dash of sugar
not too sweet, just a little treat
to wet my appetite
my chocolate lover
shackled on the ship
I ask, can we trip?
I just don't want to get caught up in the trip
but on the real tip
I was wondering..
can I play in you?

Imagination

I want to dance with the stars
drink from planet Venus
and chat about philosophy with my friends
as we let our imaginations
reach the greatest heights
I would love to lay on the beach in the Bahamas
gaze upon the vastness of the ocean
what a joy to live in Europe for a year and soak up the culture
sip cappuccino at a sidewalk café
while feeding my man kisses
and giggle at his advances
I want to greet each sunrise with a smile
and thank God I made it through yet
another day of
Imagining....

Thunder in My Bones

Cannot contain this storm
within
I scream
free me from this oppressive cage
tired, can't go on
taste of freedom
just a fantasy...someday
I will be free to arrest the
thunder in my bones
won't be long now
Spirit tells me
tears flow like a river
sweet surrender
Elohim! Abba!
open up the heavens and show me the perfect rainbows
you created when you made a covenant with
Noah
thunder in my bones
won't be long now chile
the love of the Lord covers me
lulls me into a peaceful rest
suffering is the test
endurance is blessed!
I awake to stillness in my spirit
smile upon my face
I won the battle against this...
thunder I my bones

Journey

Driving along Interstate 15
my girls and I heading for Palm Springs
I prop my feet on the dashboard in the California sun
displaying hussy red toenail polish
and joined in the laughter
chatting about ex-boyfriends...
the good, the bad and the ugly
Journey
too late for regret, no turning back
however
tucked away in the corner of my mind
you still rent space within my pretty head
am I a prisoner of my emotions?
will I ever be free?
to come out of hiding in the shadows of a relationship that was
doomed from the beginning?
Journey
to be free to fly with the birds
the mindless chatter
brings me crashing back down to earth
as the wind sings a song in my hair
and the sun coats my honey-colored skin
I can only imagine freedom
so lost in love
or what I thought was love
two people needing each other for the wrong reason
I still dance with hurt and danger

I gave up too much of myself
Journey
I pray will all my might will lead me back to me!

Menfolks

Girl, dem menfolks aint right
wanna argue, fuss and fight
sho like to poke fun at us
her feet too big
any ol excuse they wanna use
dem menfolks aint right
well girl, not all of em is bad
some good one's out there
sho love menfolks
but girlfriend
sometimes I get da blues
feel misused
once in awhile
they have to be in the streets
with other menfolks
doing what God only knows
can't leave em alone
won't leave em alone
I love me dem menfolks!

Dusk

Marveling at the beauty of God's work
I watch the sun slowly descend
behind the mountains
teasing me with its' peek-a-boo beauty
dusk ushers in a certain peace
covering the city with stillness and spectacular views
as the sun waves goodbye
I beg...
please come back
it must be God's favorite time of the day
a serene blending of red and orange hues
I wait and wait...
longing to freeze this time frame
so I can revel in it
forever!

African Violet

The ocean rises to greet her at noonday
flowers stand to salute her in the garden
Mr. Sun applauds the Queen
hand sculpted by God
the moon bows
stars marvel at her beauty
clouds wave as she passes
rainbows are in awe of her warmth
the earth, her playground
her gait, regal, enchanting
intoxicating perfume
her laughter – full of love and heard throughout the world
she is the prettiest flower on earth
the African Violet

Rhythm of a Drag

He stepped to me spitting game
with mysterious, hypnotic eyes
he possessed a funky rhythm,
mesmerizing..
we began to groove
off beat at first
so I guided him
our hips swayed back and forth
full of soul and passion
in our dance
he started to lead and along came the
DRAG
did not dig his song or music
he caught up
and left me
behind
rhythm out of sync
no chorus or melody..just da
blues
don't strut anymore, can't find anyone
to move to a groove with
aint no fun dancing alone to the
rhythm of a DRAG

In Love's Moment

        Drunk off your sweetness
        caught up
        hung up
        on you
        I fell
        around you
        behind you
        high
        under your spell
        wishing to stay in
        love's moment forever!

More than Friends, Less than Lovers

Crossing the fine line of friendship
you caressed me
while Ms. Anita Baker soothed me
are we
more than friends or less than lovers?
your fences too high to climb
I internalized this puzzle called
us
attempted to define the F word – friends
you invited me into your world
never suspecting another girl
would be having your baby
remember
when you longed to be my baby?
my devotion to the Lord confused you
the confession of love trapped me into the
private hell of secrecy
care we
more than friends or less than lovers?
your abandonment issues
rooted in fear
I searched your handsome face
noticed it tighten with anger
as I laid down the law
peeling away your manhood
layer by layer
my only defense was to hide behind the pain

and hurl hurtful accusations
are we
more than friends or less than lovers?
my tears made you retreat
I called you a coward
you returned and peeped into my soul
with a wide-eyed curiosity
questioning the intensity of our passion
what exactly are we...
more than friends or less than lovers?

Sista Maya

Your sweet diction is like sugar to my soul
how gracious and humble you are
a star
Sista Maya
soulful poetess
with a heart and dignity of a Queen
you touched my life with
"I Know why the Caged Bird Sings"
out of the tomb of ugliness came beauty
God made you better, not bitter
oh dear one
it was God's grace that covered your delicate young life
we are in awe of your dance
words curtsy around your beautiful crown
we stand on your broad shoulders
praying to capture just a touch
of your greatness
in the beauty of prose
oh Sista Maya
how deep will you take us?

Afterthought

Dig the flavors of Africa.....
chocolate, café-au-lait, honey, cappuccino, black
tar baby
but
blue
you make me
believing the hype that Blackness
equates inferiority
nappy, kinky Afros stand proud on righteous heads
that shake in disgust at the blatant rape
of Afrocentric culture
peep this...
has anyone considered the cost of Blackness?
Marvin screamed..makes me wanna holler
thirty plus years later
Missy Elliot sez....holla
why are we still shouting?
INJUSTICE perhaps?
is Afro-American/Black a trend?
is it cool to be Black?
or Black to be cool?
what exactly is Blackness?
another label...
Nu classic-Neo-soul
pleeeeezzzz...
check out how Berry Gordy groomed his artists from the
inside out

timeless soul wrapped in elegance, talent and style!
but tricky gimmicks are the norm today
who over-produce-studio-manufactured
wanna-be-so-called "singers" who steal/imitate/try-to-duplicate
African rhythm
and
will somebody please cut off those repetitive tracks
check to see if there is a note dangling....somewhere
anywhere
perhaps over the rainbow as Patti LaBelle
reaches notes only God can give
it's funny, recent Census sez......Blackness is the last thang to claim...humph
does being "half-Black" leave a bitter taste in yo mouth?
let's flip the script...again...why is
Blackness considered an
Afterthought?

Kissing my Soul

I beckon you, come closer
feel my warmth
while I sip from your chocolate soul
as you get lost in my big hips
my Prince
I offer you my soul
not to control
but to kiss,
caress
envelope my essence
as only your Afrocentric self can
come kiss my soul
and send me to new heights of
love
your hands hold my body
custom made just for you
you touch the "onion"
tell me lover
does it bring tears to your eyes?
don't cry pretty brown baby
just hold me as we melt into oneness
dig my flavor
kiss my soul
feel the comfort of my chocolate skin
as we enter the zone of love
I welcome your tar baby beauty
high cheekbones

rough, nappy hair
and oh, those big, full, lips
insight a riot of passion
within my bones
come, Nubian King
let our souls become one.....

Sweet Tears in Bitter Coffee

Laughter jumps within the deepest part of my soul
tickling delicate places
your wacky style, sunshine smile
warms my spirit
It's funny how love sneaks up in you
lurches from your womanhood
after laying dormant in the cobwebs of your heart
I weep sweet tears in bitter coffee thinking about
your gentleness
butterflies swirl in my tummy
as I examine our present dilemma
we ride it like a wave in the Pacific Ocean
storms of conflict and ghost from the past pop up
thought we buried them
I sip bitter coffee, cry sweet tears
for all the years
I've wasted
reflection purges the soul
a smile through the river of tears
appear,
make tracks down my caramel face
washing away traces of past lovers scars
I drink sweet coffee, cry bitter tears
for all the years I got caught up in a feeling
fleeing in nature
but
back to you my favorite flava...

hot-chocolate-sweetness
I've given up coffee, no more bitter tears
cause I've finally found LOVE!

Mama's Eyes

She raised four children...alone
strong, proud and full of fire
each of us a product of her passion
Mama's eyes
I see what she saw
in her children
because I too am a mother
she served us wonderful meals
at her table of honesty and courage
love sprinkled in each bit
I see hurt
surrounded by crows feet, years or pain
Mama's eyes
tell a story
dared anyone to mess with us
young fiery girl from Mississippi
no one understood her, did not try
Lula Mae, one of a kind
Mama's eyes
had to be our daddy too, wasn't easy
small backwards town gossiped about Mama
cried many tears for her beloved children
some of took wrong paths along the journey called life
Mama is special
I'm proud of her
throughout the struggles, hopes and forgotten dreams
she made it

life taught her well
the lessons are in
Mama's eyes

I Remember Love

Miss u
wish I could kiss u
hold u
until u
cling to me like a second skin
come on in
don't be afraid
I remember love, don't u
how could u be untrue
make me blue
our phone dance left me
hanging
the silence
killed me
I recall when your voice chilled me
the lies distanced us
your betrayal severed us
could not sleep last night
memories in flight
I ask God to spare me this pain
was my love in vain?
I remember love, why can't u?

I Shall Be.....

Hope
in awaiting justice for the African slave trade
my voice raises a decibel in the poetic dance
attempting to silence the screams of
Kings and Queens from the grave of the abyss
I shall be..
Fire
a silent passion burns within for our future generation
who will save the babies?
I shall be...
Rain
a soft, delicate mist slowly descending upon my man
whispering "I love you"
while opening my heart to embrace togetherness
I shall be...
Peace
a quiet, Godly strength, meekness covers my soul
stillness my coat
I shall be...
many things for many reasons
as my seasons change
moody blue
or whether I'm smiling at the sunset
I shall be...
Great!
Bold!
with a flair for life

a touch of grace with loads of humility
I shall be...
a Christian, humanitarian, poet, writer, mother, wife,
friend, daughter, granddaughter, sister, aunt, cousin,
niece..
I shall be...
a woman of dignity and character
with head held up by graying temples and crows feet
I shall be..
the life of grandmother's wrinkled hands
that picked cotton, held a pistol, prepared meals,
while raising chillen through clenched fists holding
onto regrets
I shall be...
some of what life has molded
love has scolded
what God has corrected
and made stronger
I shall be...-
the jazz and blues combined
soft and sassy
as I ride upon the melody
of rhythm and blues
I shall be...
all I can be according to
His purpose!

Lover's Point

Cant recall if it was the cold wind or our attraction
that gave me chills
I found comfort in your big arms
all one hundred eighty pounds of you
wrapped in a blanket of forbidden lust
the ocean offered solitude
nestled in the hills of Carmel
Lover's Point
our cozy meeting place
I reflect how your deep, delicious dimples framed
your handsome face
along with a muscular body that screams 100%
man
we made promises neither of us would keep
I return to Lover's Point
alone
as the sand slips through my fingers
so did our love
oh, how I yearn for your arms once again
memories of us beckons a smile
as I gaze at the splendor of Lover's Point
I wonder....
Where are you now?

October

I remember the cool, crisp October breeze
the month of our break up
Recalling how the sun settled so peacefully in your living room
my spirit was as rest
while the walls eavesdropped on our intimate conversations
so long ago
now it's the end of summer
can't face it
the beginning of October
hate it
wearing your oversized sweater
tucked away in our corner of the world
 like I belonged
so I thought....
remember last October?
when I found lipstick traces
foolish me
 love has no guarantees
and baby
you are not worth my sanity
I must hold on and not fall to pieces
remember last October
wish I could forget!

Lost in You

My places and spaces are filled with dreams of us
remembering the magic of love
and the stillness of my heart
unable to breath
only your sweet air filled my lungs
my soul at peace
I found a resting place
in you
but
I stayed in you too long
now you're gone
 I wish you was still a part of my life
so we could get lost
together

Essence

We cry
we laugh
we shout
we sing
we reach
we swing
we clap
we dream
we fall
we wish
we create
we wait
we play
we hurt
we flirt
we soar
we hope
we love
We Women!

Dear Readers,

   Thank you for purchasing Afterthought...I've included the following journal pages for your reflections.
   Feel free to express yourself, jot down ideas for a poetry book of your own......the world awaits your greatness.

Peace and Blessings!
Linda

Now Write Your Poems Here

Now Write Your Poems Here

Now Write Your Poems Here

Now Write Your Poems Here

Now Write Your Poems Here

Now Write Your Poems Here

www.ingramcontent.com/pod-product-compliance
Lightning Source LLC
Chambersburg PA
CBHW020023050426
42450CB00005B/623